Prayer and Reflection Journal for Educators

April Short

-Scripture Readings
-Reflection
-Prayer
(Located in the back of the journal)

This Journal Belongs to:

Date:

Scripture Reading: Proverbs 9:9
Instruct the wise and they will be wiser
still; teach the righteous and they will
add to their learning.

Reflect:

_____

_____

_____

_____

_____

_____

_____

_____

_____

Date:

Scripture Reading: Proverbs 22:6
Train up a child in the way he should go;
even when he is old he will not depart
from it.

Reflect:

_____

_____

_____

_____

_____

_____

_____

_____

Date:

Scripture Reading: Matthew 28:20
And teaching them to obey everything I have commanded you. And surely I am with you always, to the very end of the age.

Reflect:

_____

_____

_____

_____

_____

_____

_____

_____

Date:

Scripture Reading: Romans 12:6-7
We have different gifts, according to the grace given to each of us. If your gift is prophesying, then prophesy in accordance with your faith; if it is serving, then serve; if it is teaching, then teach.

Reflect:

_____

_____

_____

_____

_____

_____

_____

_____

Date:

Scripture Reading: Romans 15:4
For everything that was written in the past was written to teach us, so that through the endurance taught in the Scriptures and the encouragement they provide we might have hope.

Reflect:

_____

_____

_____

_____

_____

_____

_____

_____

_____

Date:

Scripture Reading: Galatians 5:22-23
But the fruit of the Spirit is love, joy, peace, longsuffering, gentleness, goodness, faith, meekness, temperance: against such there is no law.

Reflect:

_____

_____

_____

_____

_____

_____

_____

_____

Date:

Scripture Reading: 1 Peter 3:15
But in your hearts revere Christ as Lord.
Always be prepared to give an answer to
everyone who asks you to give the reason
for the hope that you have. But do this
with gentleness and respect.

Reflect:

_____

_____

_____

_____

_____

_____

_____

_____

_____

Date:

Scripture Reading: Proverbs 3:5-6
Trust in the LORD with all your heart,
and lean not on your own
understanding; in all your ways
acknowledge Him, and He shall direct
your paths.

Reflect:

_____

_____

_____

_____

_____

_____

_____

_____

Date:

Scripture Reading: Psalms 32:8
I will instruct you and teach you in the way you should go; I will counsel you with my loving eye on you.

Reflect:

_____

_____

_____

_____

_____

_____

_____

_____

Date:

Scripture Reading: Proverbs 16:23-24
The hearts of the wise make their mouths prudent, and their lips promote instruction. Gracious words are a honeycomb, sweet to the soul and healing to the bones.

Reflect:

_____

_____

_____

_____

_____

_____

_____

_____

Date:

Scripture Reading: Deuteronomy 32:2
Let my teaching fall like rain and my
words descend like dew, like showers
on new grass, like abundant rain on
tender plants.

Reflect:

_____

_____

_____

_____

_____

_____

_____

_____

Date:

Scripture Reading: Jeremiah 17:8
They shall be like a tree planted by water,
sending out its roots by the stream.
It shall not fear when heat comes,
and its leaves shall stay green;
in the year of drought it is not anxious,
and it does not cease to bear fruit.

Reflect:

_____

_____

_____

_____

_____

_____

_____

_____

Date:

Scripture Reading: 1 John 2:27
As for you, the anointing you received from him remains in you, and you do not need anyone to teach you. But as his anointing teaches you about all things and as that anointing is real, not counterfeit—just as it has taught you, remain in him.

Reflect:

_____

_____

_____

_____

_____

_____

_____

_____

_____

Date:

Scripture Reading: 1 Corinthians 12:28
And God has placed in the church first of
all apostles, second prophets, third
teachers, then miracles, then gifts of
healing, of helping, of guidance, and of
different kinds of tongues.

Reflect:

_____

_____

_____

_____

_____

_____

_____

_____

Date:

Scripture Reading: 1 Samuel 12:23
Moreover as for me, God forbid that I
should sin against the LORD in ceasing
to pray for you: but I will teach you the
good and the right way.

Reflect:

_____

_____

_____

_____

_____

_____

_____

_____

Date:

Scripture Reading: Luke 6:40
The student is not above the teacher,
but everyone who is fully trained will
be like their teacher.

Reflect:

_____

_____

_____

_____

_____

_____

_____

_____

Date:

Scripture Reading: Corinthians 15:58
Therefore, my dear brothers and sisters, stand firm. Let nothing move you. Always give yourselves fully to the work of the Lord, because you know that your labor in the Lord is not in vain.

Reflect:

_____

_____

_____

_____

_____

_____

_____

_____

Date:

Scripture Reading: 1 Chronicles 25:8
Young and old alike, teacher as well
as student, cast lots for their duties.

Reflect:

_____

_____

_____

_____

_____

_____

_____

_____

Date:

Scripture Reading: Galatians 6:6
Nevertheless, the one who receives instruction in the word should share all good things with their instructor.

Reflect:

_____

_____

_____

_____

_____

_____

_____

_____

_____

Date:

Scripture Reading: Colossians 3:16
Let the message of Christ dwell among
you richly as you teach and admonish
one another with all wisdom through
psalms, hymns, and songs from the
Spirit, singing to God with gratitude in
your hearts.   ## Reflect:

_____

_____

_____

_____

_____

_____

_____

_____

Date:

Scripture Reading: Titus 2:7-8

In everything set them an example by doing what is good. In your teaching show integrity, seriousness and soundness of speech that cannot be condemned, so that those who oppose you may be ashamed because they have nothing bad to say about us.

Reflect:

_____

_____

_____

_____

_____

_____

_____

_____

_____

Date:

Scripture Reading: James 1:5
If any of you lacks wisdom, you should
ask God, who gives generously to all
without finding fault, and it will be given
to you.

Reflect:

_____

_____

_____

_____

_____

_____

_____

_____

Date:

Scripture Reading: Titus 2:3-5

Likewise, teach the older women to be reverent in the way they live, not to be slanderers or addicted to much wine, but to teach what is good. Then they can urge the younger women to love their husbands and children, to be self-controlled and pure, to be busy at home, to be kind, and to be subject to their husbands, so that no one will malign the word of God.

Reflect:

_____

_____

_____

_____

_____

_____

_____

_____

_____

Date:

Scripture Reading: Luke 11: 1 – 4

And it came to pass, that, as he was praying in a certain place, when he ceased, one of his disciples said unto him, Lord, teach us to pray, as John also taught his disciples. And he said unto them, When ye pray, say, Our Father which art in heaven, Hallowed be thy name. Thy kingdom come. Thy will be done, as in heaven, so in earth. Give us day by day our daily bread. And forgive us our sins; for we also forgive every one that is indebted to us. And lead us not into temptation; but deliver us from evil.

Reflect:

_____

_____

_____

_____

_____

_____

_____

_____

Date:

Scripture Reading: 1 Peter 4:10
Like good stewards of the manifold grace of God, serve one another with whatever gift each of you has received.

Reflect:

_____

_____

_____

_____

_____

_____

_____

Date:

Scripture Reading: Deuteronomy 11:18-19
Fix these words of mine in your hearts and minds; tie them as symbols on your hands and bind them on your foreheads. Teach them to your children, talking about them when you sit at home and when you walk along the road, when you lie down and when you get up.

Reflect:

_____

_____

_____

_____

_____

_____

_____

_____

Date:

Scripture Reading: Proverbs 1:2-4
For gaining wisdom and instruction;
for understanding words of insight;
for receiving instruction in prudent behavior,
doing what is right and just and fair;
for giving prudence to those who are simple,
knowledge and discretion to the young.

Reflect:

_____

_____

_____

_____

_____

_____

_____

_____

Date:

Scripture Reading: Matthew 10:24
The student is not above the teacher,
nor a servant above his master.

Reflect:

_____

_____

_____

_____

_____

_____

_____

_____

Date:

Scripture Reading: 2 Timothy 1:11
"And of this gospel I was appointed a
herald and an apostle and a teacher."

Reflect:

_____

_____

_____

_____

_____

_____

_____

_____

Date:

Scripture Reading: Philippians 4:13
I can do all this through him who gives
me strength.

Reflect:

_____

_____

_____

_____

_____

_____

_____

_____

_____

Date:

Scripture Reading: 1 Timothy 4:11
Teach these things and insist that
everyone learn them.

Reflect:

_____

_____

_____

_____

_____

_____

_____

_____

_____

Date:

Scripture Reading: Psalm 37:30
The mouths of the righteous utter
wisdom, and their tongues speak what
is just.

Reflect:

_____

_____

_____

_____

_____

_____

_____

_____

Date:

Scripture Reading: Exodus 4:12
Now go; I will help you speak and will teach you what to say.

Reflect:

_____

_____

_____

_____

_____

_____

_____

_____

_____

Date:

Scripture Reading: Deuteronomy 31:6
Be strong and courageous. Do not fear
or be in dread of them, for it is the
LORD your God who goes with you. He
will not leave you or forsake you.

✝   Reflect:

_____

_____

_____

_____

_____

_____

_____

_____

Date:

Scripture Reading: Luke 12:12
For "the Holy Spirit will teach you in
that very hour what you ought to say."

Reflect:

_____

_____

_____

_____

_____

_____

_____

_____

Date:

Scripture Reading: 2 Timothy 1:7
For God hath not given us the spirit of fear; but of power, and of love, and of a sound mind.

Reflect:

_____

_____

_____

_____

_____

_____

_____

_____

Date:

Scripture Reading: 2 Timothy 2:15
Do your best to present yourself to God
as one approved, a worker who does
not need to be ashamed and who
correctly handles the word of truth.

Reflect:

_____

_____

_____

_____

_____

_____

_____

_____

Date:

Scripture Reading: Romans 2:21
Well then, if you teach others, why
don't you teach yourself? You tell
others not to steal, but do you steal?

Reflect:

_____

_____

_____

_____

_____

_____

_____

_____

Date:

Scripture Reading: Luke 2:45-46

When they did not find him, they went back to Jerusalem to look for him. After three days they found him in the temple courts, sitting among the teachers, listening to them and asking them questions.

Reflect:

_____

_____

_____

_____

_____

_____

_____

_____

Date:

Scripture Reading: John 13:13
"You call me Teacher and Lord, and you are right, because that's what I am."

Reflect:

_____

_____

_____

_____

_____

_____

_____

_____

Date:

Scripture Reading: John 11:28
After she had said this, she went back and called her sister Mary aside. "The Teacher is here," she said, "and is asking for you.

Reflect:

_____

_____

_____

_____

_____

_____

_____

_____

_____

Date:

Scripture Reading: John 3:10
Jesus answered and said to him, are
you the teacher of Israel and do not
understand these things?

Reflect:

_____

_____

_____

_____

_____

_____

_____

_____

_____

Date:

Scripture Reading: Galatians 6:9
Let's not be weary in doing good, for we will reap in due season, if we don't give up.

Reflect:

_____

_____

_____

_____

_____

_____

_____

_____

_____

Date:

Scripture Reading: Matthew 19:14
But Jesus said, Allow the little children,
and don't forbid them to come to me;
for the Kingdom of Heaven belongs to
ones like these.

Reflect:

_____

_____

_____

_____

_____

_____

_____

_____

Date:

Scripture Reading: Matthew 5:19
Therefore anyone who sets aside one of the least of these commands and teaches others accordingly will be called least in the kingdom of heaven, but whoever practices and teaches these commands will be called great in the kingdom of heaven.

Reflect:

_____

_____

_____

_____

_____

_____

_____

_____

Date:

Scripture Reading:1 Chronicles 25:8
Young and old alike, teacher as well as
student, cast lots for their duties.

Reflect:

_____

_____

_____

_____

_____

_____

_____

_____

_____

Date:

Scripture Reading: James 3:1-2

Not many of you should become teachers, my fellow believers, because you know that we who teach will be judged more strictly. We all stumble in many ways. Anyone who is never at fault in what they say is perfect, able to keep their whole body in check.

Reflect:

_____

_____

_____

_____

_____

_____

_____

_____

Date:

Scripture Reading: Hebrews 5:12

For though by this time you ought to be teachers, you have need again for someone to teach you the elementary principles of the oracles of God, and you have come to need milk and not solid food.

Reflect:

_____

_____

_____

_____

_____

_____

_____

_____

Date:

Scripture Reading: Ephesians 4:11
And He gave some as apostles, and
some as prophets, and some as
evangelists, and some as pastors and
teachers.

Reflect:

_____

_____

_____

_____

_____

_____

_____

_____

Date:

Scripture Reading: 1 Corinthians 12:29
All are not apostles, are they? All are not prophets, are they? All are not teachers, are they? All are not workers of miracles, are they?

Reflect:

_____

_____

_____

_____

_____

_____

_____

_____

Date:

Scripture Reading: Psalm 119:99
I have more insight than all my
teachers, for your testimonies are my
meditation.

Reflect:

_____

_____

_____

_____

_____

_____

_____

_____

Date:

Scripture Reading: Proverbs 5:13
I have not listened to the voice of my teachers, Nor inclined my ear to my instructors!

Reflect:

_____

_____

_____

_____

_____

_____

_____

_____

Date:

Scripture Reading: 2 Timothy 2:24
The Lord's bond-servant must not be quarrelsome, but be kind to all, able to teach, patient when wronged.

Reflect:

_____

_____

_____

_____

_____

_____

_____

_____

Date:

Scripture Reading: 1 Timothy 2:12
But I do not allow a woman to teach or
exercise authority over a man, but to
remain quiet.

Reflect:

_____

_____

_____

_____

_____

_____

_____

_____

Date:

Scripture Reading: Romans 2:20
A corrector of the foolish, a teacher of
the immature, having in the law the
embodiment of knowledge and of the
truth.

Reflect:

_____

_____

_____

_____

_____

_____

_____

_____

Date:

Scripture Reading: 1 Timothy 6:3
If anyone advocates a different doctrine
and does not agree with sound words,
those of our Lord Jesus Christ, and with
the doctrine conforming to godliness.

Reflect:

_____

_____

_____

_____

_____

_____

_____

_____

Date:

Scripture Reading: John 7:16
So Jesus answered them and said, "My teaching is not Mine, but His who sent Me.

Reflect:

_____

_____

_____

_____

_____

_____

_____

_____

_____

Date:

Scripture Reading: Matthew 23:8
But do not be called Rabbi; for one is
your teacher, and you are all brothers.

Reflect:

_____

_____

_____

_____

_____

_____

_____

_____

Date:

Scripture Reading: 2 Timothy 3:16
All Scripture is inspired by God and
profitable for teaching, for reproof, for
correction, for training in righteousness.

Reflect:

_____

_____

_____

_____

_____

_____

_____

_____

Date:

Scripture Reading: John 14:26
But the Helper, the Holy Spirit, whom
the Father will send in My name, He will
teach you all things, and bring to your
remembrance all that I said to you.

Reflect:

_____

_____

_____

_____

_____

_____

_____

_____

_____

Date:

Prayer

_____

_____

_____

_____

_____

_____

_____

_____

_____

_____

Date:

Prayer

_____

_____

_____

_____

_____

_____

_____

_____

_____

_____

Date:

Prayer

_____

_____

_____

_____

_____

_____

_____

_____

_____

Date:

Prayer

_____

_____

_____

_____

_____

_____

_____

_____

_____

_____

Date:

Prayer

_____

_____

_____

_____

_____

_____

_____

_____

_____

_____

Date:

Prayer

_____

_____

_____

_____

_____

_____

_____

_____

_____

Date:

Prayer

_____

_____

_____

_____

_____

_____

_____

_____

_____

Date:

Prayer

_____

_____

_____

_____

_____

_____

_____

_____

_____

Date:

Prayer

_____

_____

_____

_____

_____

_____

_____

_____

_____

Date:

Prayer

_____

_____

_____

_____

_____

_____

_____

_____

_____

_____

Date:

Prayer

_____

_____

_____

_____

_____

_____

_____

_____

_____

Date:

Prayer

_____

_____

_____

_____

_____

_____

_____

_____

_____

_____

Date:

Prayer

_____

_____

_____

_____

_____

_____

_____

_____

_____

Date:

Prayer

_____

_____

_____

_____

_____

_____

_____

_____

_____

_____

Date:

Prayer

_____

_____

_____

_____

_____

_____

_____

_____

_____

Date:

Prayer

_____

_____

_____

_____

_____

_____

_____

_____

_____

_____

Date:

Prayer

_____

_____

_____

_____

_____

_____

_____

_____

_____

Date:

Prayer

_____

_____

_____

_____

_____

_____

_____

_____

_____

_____

Date:

Prayer

_____

_____

_____

_____

_____

_____

_____

_____

_____

_____

Date:

Prayer

_____

_____

_____

_____

_____

_____

_____

_____

_____

Date:

Prayer

_____

_____

_____

_____

_____

_____

_____

_____

_____

_____

Date:

Prayer

_____

_____

_____

_____

_____

_____

_____

_____

_____

_____

Date:

Prayer

_____

_____

_____

_____

_____

_____

_____

_____

_____

Date:

Prayer

_____

_____

_____

_____

_____

_____

_____

_____

_____

_____

Date:

Prayer

_____

_____

_____

_____

_____

_____

_____

_____

_____

Date:

Prayer

_____

_____

_____

_____

_____

_____

_____

_____

_____

_____

Date:

Prayer

_____

_____

_____

_____

_____

_____

_____

_____

_____

_____

Date:

Prayer

_____

_____

_____

_____

_____

_____

_____

_____

_____

_____

Date:

Prayer

_____

_____

_____

_____

_____

_____

_____

_____

_____

Date:

Prayer

_____

_____

_____

_____

_____

_____

_____

_____

_____

_____

Date:

Prayer

_____

_____

_____

_____

_____

_____

_____

_____

_____

Date:

Prayer

_____

_____

_____

_____

_____

_____

_____

_____

_____

_____

Date:

Prayer

_____

_____

_____

_____

_____

_____

_____

_____

_____

_____

Date:

Prayer

_____

_____

_____

_____

_____

_____

_____

_____

_____

_____

Date:

Prayer

_____

_____

_____

_____

_____

_____

_____

_____

_____

_____

Date:

Prayer

_____

_____

_____

_____

_____

_____

_____

_____

_____

_____

Date:

Prayer

_____

_____

_____

_____

_____

_____

_____

_____

_____

_____

Date:

Prayer

_____

_____

_____

_____

_____

_____

_____

_____

_____

_____

Date:

Prayer

_____

_____

_____

_____

_____

_____

_____

_____

_____

Made in the USA
Middletown, DE
08 August 2022